★SKILLS BUILDERS

Reading Comprehension

LEVELS 5–7

Marie Lallaway, Tom Johns and Mig Bennett

Rising Stars UK Ltd, 22 Grafton Street, London W1S 4EX

www.risingstars-uk.com

Published 2010

Text, design and layout © 2008 Rising Stars UK Ltd.

Editorial: Sandra Stafford
Illustrations: Phill Burrows
Design: Branford Graphics and Clive Sutherland
Cover design: Burville-Riley Partnership

Text acknowledgements

pp6–7 Extracts from *Ray Mears Bushcraft Survival* by Ray Mears; pp12–13 Extract from *Great Expectations* by Charles Dickens; p14 Extract from *The Kite Rider* by Geraldine McCaughrean, Oxford University Press; pp18–19 Extract from *The Speckled Band* by Sir Arthur Conan Doyle; p20 Extract from *A Walk in the Woods* by Bill Bryson; p24 Extract from *Spilled Water* by Sally Grindley, Bloomsbury; p25 Extract from *Powder Monkey* by Paul Dowswell, Bloomsbury; pp26–27 Extract from *The Wereling: Wounded* by Stephen Cole, Bloomsbury; p30 Extract from *Great Expectations* by Charles Dickens; p31 Extract from *Frankenstein* by Mary Shelley; p32 Extract from *Animal Farm* by George Orwell; p33 'How to invest in collectible toys' The Times; p34 Extract from *The Tell-Tale Heart* by Edgar Allen Poe; p35 Extract from *Hunted* by N.M. Browne, Bloomsbury; p38 *Boy* by Roald Dahl. Reproduced by permission of Jonathon Cape Ltd & Penguin Books Ltd.; pp40–41 Extract from *The Other Side of the Dale* by Gervase Phinn; p42 Extract from *An Indian Boy's Story* by An-nen-la-de-ni, University of Virginia; pp44–45 Extract from *Next Term, We'll Mash You* by Penelope Lively, Penguin

Picture acknowledgements

p6 Kevin Arnold/The Image Bank/Getty Images; p8 Suzann Julien/iStockphoto; p12 BFI; p18 Headhunters/Getty Images; p28 Paul Gilham/Getty Images; p30 BFI; p31 Sygma/Corbis; p33 Steve Gorton/Dorling Kindersley/Getty Images; p36 Gray Mortimore/Allsport/Getty Images; p37 David Madison/Corbis

British Library Cataloguing in Publication Data.
A CIP record for this book is available from the British Library.

ISBN: 978 1 84680 683 4

Printed by Craft Print International Ltd, Singapore

Contents

What are reading skills?

Working at Level 5, you may already know that reading skills include the different ways that you are expected to respond to a text.

These skills are called 'assessment focuses' (AFs) and your teacher considers how well you can perform them when assessing your National Curriculum level for reading.

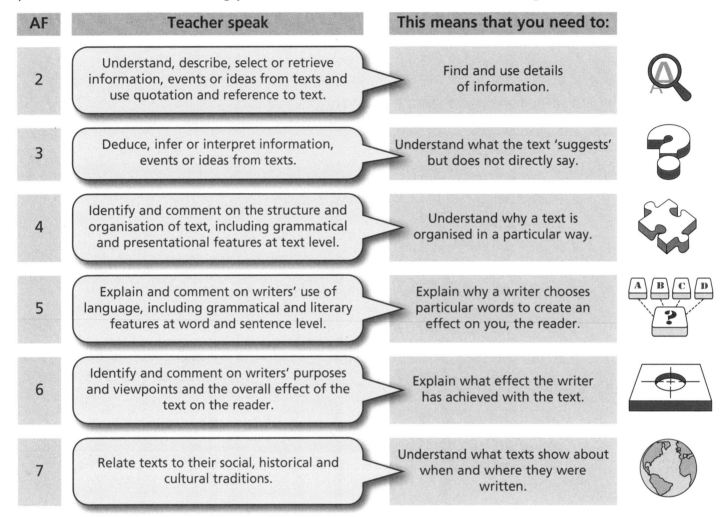

AF	Teacher speak	This means that you need to:
2	Understand, describe, select or retrieve information, events or ideas from texts and use quotation and reference to text.	Find and use details of information.
3	Deduce, infer or interpret information, events or ideas from texts.	Understand what the text 'suggests' but does not directly say.
4	Identify and comment on the structure and organisation of text, including grammatical and presentational features at text level.	Understand why a text is organised in a particular way.
5	Explain and comment on writers' use of language, including grammatical and literary features at word and sentence level.	Explain why a writer chooses particular words to create an effect on you, the reader.
6	Identify and comment on writers' purposes and viewpoints and the overall effect of the text on the reader.	Explain what effect the writer has achieved with the text.
7	Relate texts to their social, historical and cultural traditions.	Understand what texts show about when and where they were written.

Why use this book?

This book will help you to move your reading skills up from one National Curriculum level to another. For example, if you are currently working at level 5, advice and exercises will help you to progress to level 6, or 7.

- **Knowing what you need to do** to achieve your target level is also essential so we explain and give examples of what you need to be able to do.
- We know that students **learn by doing** so practice is an important part of the book.

The book includes the following features to make it easy to use and to highlight what you really need to be able to do.

Target level statement – this tells you what you need to do to achieve the next level in your reading skill.

Assessment focus – this identifies the main reading skill that is being practised. See page 5 for more information.

Tips – these give you helpful hints, similar to how your teacher does in class.

Practice questions – lots of short fiction and non-fiction texts with guided questions for you to practise with and build your skills and confidence in reading.

How to use this book

- You can use the sections in this book to work on the reading skills you need to practise. Or, work through the whole book for overall improvement.

- Each section targets a different reading skill and allows you to practise the skill in a variety of ways across levels 5, 6 and 7 so that you can learn the 'extra' things you need to understand and do for each level.

- Practise in short bursts of activity and **do** read the advice first so that you focus on the reading skill, not just answering the questions.

- Continue your practice by thinking of your own questions about the things you read outside of this book. For example, when reading a news article, think about what you could ask someone else about it.

Use this table to identify what you want to do first.

Reading skills	Find and use details of information	Understand what the text 'suggests' but does not directly say	Understand why a text is organised in a particular way	Explain why a writer chooses particular words to create an effect on you, the reader	Explain what effect the writer has achieved with the text
Level 5	find details from larger amounts of text and use them as evidence to support opinions	explain the writer's meanings in your own words	identify the pattern of ideas in a text and make comments about it	identify and comment on the effects of interesting language	identify the purpose of a text and begin to explain its effect on the reader
Level 6	find relevant information from different places in a text to provide a summary or support an opinion	find deeper meanings and begin to explain them using details to support your answers	identify and comment on how the text is organised	comment in some detail on a writer's choice of language	explain, using quotations and references, the effect of the text on the reader
Level 7	select precise information to support research and argument	interpret meanings from what is said and unsaid in a text	evaluate the effect of some features of text organisation	analyse the writer's language for its effect	analyse how a writer's viewpoint and purpose are presented and developed

Finding and using information in a text

Level 5 readers can find information from large amounts of text, and find evidence to support opinions.

Level 6 readers can find relevant information from different places in a text to provide a summary or to support opinions.

TIP ★ Highlighting and underlining are useful ways of keeping track of evidence.

1 Read this text by television presenter Ray Mears about his experience of 'real' life with a tribe in East Africa.

Our campsite was in the heart of Masai country, where the rolling hills provide plenty of lush pasture for their cattle. Throughout the year, the Masai, the largest tribe in Tanzania, travel in small groups, and they live almost entirely on the meat and milk of their herds. The guide for my two-day trek through this stunning landscape was a warrior called Mtele, who had an intimate knowledge of the area, and as we were heading into big-game country, we had also arranged for an experienced, armed ranger to travel with us.

Before setting out, each of us prepared our individual supplies for the trip. For Mtele this meant cutting out the lining of a goat's stomach and filling it with the animal's meat and fat before 'vacuum-sealing' it with a small strip of bark and some wooden pegs. His only other equipment was a sword, a spear and a stick to which he attached his pouch of food. Mtele provided a shining example of how to travel light in the wilderness and although my preparations were slightly different, I too had only a modest amount of kit with me in addition to my ready-prepared rations. I also took a water purifier, which is essential for anyone who is not local, and a sleeping bag because it can get fairly cold under the cloudless skies of Africa.

Ray Mears Bushcraft Survival by Ray Mears

Decide if statements a) and b) are True or False. Draw arrows to the information in the text that gave the answers.

a) The Masai are the smallest tribe in Tanzania.   **True** ☐   **False** ☑

b) The Masai's only food is their cattle.   **True** ☑   **False** ☐

These were fairly easy statements to decide on because each answer could be found in one place. The next statement needs three lines to the text to bring together three bits of information for a correct answer.

c) The Masai landscape is flat, ugly and desert.   **True** ☐   **False** ☑

2 Scan ALL the text on page 6 to find the information you need to answer a) and b).

a) Give two reasons why Mears had Mtele and a ranger with him on his safari.

(To protect him.) He took them because they had great Rangle knoledle, and they had essential equipment.

b) Give three reasons why Mears took along a water purifier but Mtele didn't.

Mears took along a water purifier because he's not local. Mtele didn't need it because he's local.

3 Read the next part of Ray Mears' account.

Later in the day we began to look for a site to set up camp in good time as night falls quickly in this region. We were camping Masai style which meant no tents or modern equipment of any description, just the vegetation we could find near our chosen site. I am always fascinated to see how different cultures go about organising their camp and this was the first time I had seen how the Masai sleep safely in the bush away from the village. You need protection at night from the hyenas and cheetahs, and other predators that roam this region. Your first line of defence is a fire, which will also serve as a source of heat, light and general comfort. Wild animals do not like smoke or fire and they will generally tend to turn tail at the sight or smell of it. The fire, Mtele explained, is not just a deterrent to predators, but also a beacon for fellow journeymen in the area which can be seen for miles around.

Ray Mears Bushcraft Survival by Ray Mears

Explain five reasons why fire is an important part of setting up camp for the night in Masai country.

1) *gives you heat*
2) *protection from dangerous animals*
3) *give you general comfort*
4) *At night, it gives you defence*
5) *give you source of light*

necessary

4 Walking and camping in the territory of the American Black Bear is popular but dangerous. Read the advice about how to camp safely in bear territory.

TIP ★ Read the text first, then think about the question. Go back to the text to pick out the information you need.

 Don't pitch your tents near bear food sources (fruit bushes or trees, rubbish dumps, dead animals) or where you can see bear tracks or bear claw marks on trees.

 Pitch tents in a line or semi-circle. That makes a bear easier to spot if it wanders into the site and gives it an easy escape route.

 Don't cook, eat or store food (including chocolate, sweets or their wrappers) in or close to your tents. Avoid using canned foods with strong odours (e.g. tuna, sardines). Wash out any food cans after use.

 Keep food in bear-resistant storage containers. Always store food away from the camp.

5 Look at diagrams A–C. Tick the camp site that has been set up correctly.

A
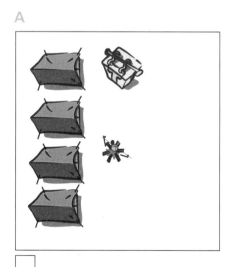
☐

B
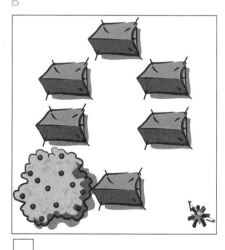
☐

C
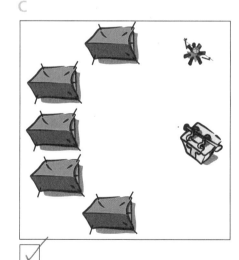
☑

6 There are other ways of trying to keep food away from bears. This diagram gives the correct information.

a) Which instruction (A or B) gives information that matches the diagram? AB

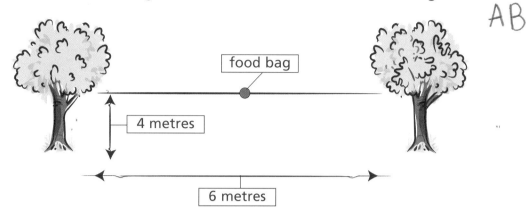

food bag

4 metres

6 metres

A

If you don't have a bear-proof container or vehicle, place food inside several layers of sealed plastic bags (to reduce odour) and put that inside a water-proof bag. If only one tree ʳ sling your bag over ̄ about 4 metreˢ that it hᵃˑ mᵃⁱ ⁿ b t

B

If you don't have a bear-proof container or vehicle, place food inside several layers of sealed plastic bags (to reduce odour) and put that inside a water-proof bag. If only one tree is available, sling your bag over a branch that is about 4 metres from ground level so that it hangs at least 1.5 metres from the main trunk. Or, find two trees about 6 metres apart and hang the bag between them at least 4 metres from the ground using nylon cord.

b) Read these frequently-asked questions about travelling in bear country. Then match one answer to each question. One has been done for you.

Frequently asked questions	Answer
1 If a bear stands on its hind legs, is it preparing to charge?	D
2 Is a bear's sense of smell better than a dog's?	B
3 Are bears naturally aggressive towards humans?	E
4 Is running the best way to escape from an aggressive bear?	D
5 Does running downhill give you a better chance of escaping from a bear?	**A**
6 If you walk in bear country, is it best to make a noise to warn off the bears?	F

A No. Bears can run faster than any human – in any direction!

B Yes. Bears have one of the most sensitive noses in the animal world.

C No. In that posture a bear is usually trying to identify you by scent or sight.

D No. Bears can run as fast as a racehorse for short distances.

E No. They are shy creatures that only act aggressively when threatened or surprised.

F Yes. That will give it time to move out of your way without feeling threatened.

9

Level 6 readers can find relevant information from different places in a text to provide a summary or to support opinions.

Level 7 readers can select precise and relevant information to support research and argument

TIP

★ Quickly read the text to get a general idea of what it is about. Then hunt for the information you need.

7 a) Scan this fact file about the famous footballer David Beckham to find how many football clubs he has played for in Europe.

Signing as a trainee for Manchester United in 1991, David Beckham was taking his first steps down the road to footballing celebrity. Born in London in 1975, he grew up with parents who, though recognising his talent, could have had no idea that he would sign as a full professional for not one, but two world-class clubs: Manchester United in 1993, and Real Madrid in 2003.

His star quality emerged when he won a footballing skills competition for under 12s at a soccer school organised by the ex-Manchester United player Bobby Charlton. The prize was two weeks of training with famous Spanish club Barcelona, so 1986 must have been doubly memorable for the young Beckham! Then he was spotted by a Manchester United scout while playing for Waltham Forest under 12s. After some years visiting and training with United, he decided to sign for them as soon as he was old enough to attain trainee status. The following year he was a member of their Youth Cup winning team, and he made his senior team debut, before eventually signing as a full professional in January 1993. He would play 311 games, score 74 goals and win 11 medals before joining Spanish giants, Real Madrid.

b) Read the text again, then fill in the missing dates and information on the timeline.

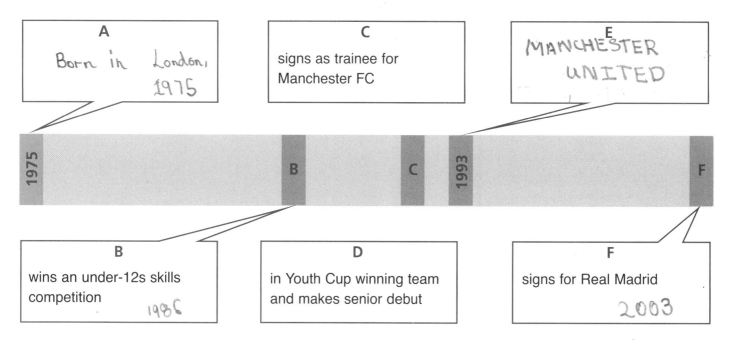

A
Born in London, 1975

C
signs as trainee for Manchester FC

E
MANCHESTER UNITED

B
wins an under-12s skills competition   1986

D
in Youth Cup winning team and makes senior debut

F
signs for Real Madrid   2003

8 Read this text from a celebrity website where readers can add their comments in a discussion forum.

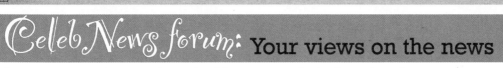

Celeb News forum: **Your views on the news**

Summer Storm has just launched her new website based on her new house. The site is a tour around a fantasy version of her mansion and it has an online chat forum for site users. 'It is fun but there's a disturbing element of exploitation of her son, Brook,' wrote CelebNews Online Editor.

WHAT DO YOU THINK?
POST YOUR COMMENTS HERE:

I think it is very sad when someone with the Summer Storm's lifestyle can put her little boy, Brook, in the spotlight like that. I think she will regret doing this, and should edit it out. Apart from that, it's fun to explore, but expensive. Oh yes, her new single gets lots of publicity!
Diane

[handwritten annotations: communication channel · Good It is fun · Bad about son · expensive]

a) Find two good points and two bad points about the site, according to the writer above.

b) Now read these comments from the website and the summaries. Match the people making the comments with the relevant summary.

Summary of comment	Comments
i) Feels it's a very successful publicity stunt. Name: *Simonia*	I am no fan, but I think it's a good idea to build a communication channel to connect a popstar directly to her audience. It's a site for people who are interested in Summer Storm, not people who don't like her. Simona
ii) Likes the site but sees a fault with it. Name: *Anna*	It is a chronic exploitation of kids who don't have credit cards but do have pre-pay mobile phones. It charges £1.50 a pop for a password that runs out after 15 days and then it's another £1.50 phonecall to get a new password! I'm sure Summer Storm will make a lovely heap of cash! Tony
iii) Thinks it's just a heartless way to make money. Name: *Tony*	I think most of the people writing in are missing the point. You all looked at it, thought about it, may have even paid for a password, and probably clicked to listen to her new single. You might not like Summer Storm but she got you, didn't she? The woman wants to sell her record for heaven's sake! Anna

TIP

★ Check the **details** of each opinion before you make your choice.

At this level you will need to show that you can collect and compare information from different areas of a text and sum up the main ideas.
The texts might be challenging, so you may need to read them twice.

9   Read this extract from the novel *Great Expectations* by Charles Dickens. The narrator is Pip, a young boy. Here, he describes his first meeting with a rich lady who has summoned him to visit her.

In an arm-chair, with an elbow resting on the table and her head leaning on that hand, sat the strangest lady I have ever seen, or shall ever see.

She was dressed in rich materials – satins, and lace, and silks – all of white. Her shoes were white. And she had a long white veil dependent from her hair, and she had bridal flowers in her hair, but her hair was white. Some bright jewels sparkled on her neck and on her hands, and some other jewels lay sparkling on the table. Dresses, less splendid than the dress she wore, and half-packed trunks, were scattered about.

She had not quite finished dressing, for she had but one shoe on – the other was on the table near her hand – her veil was but half arranged, her watch and chain were not put on, and some lace for her bosom lay with those trinkets, and with her handkerchief, and gloves, and some flowers, and a Prayer-book, all confusedly heaped about the looking-glass.

> TIP
> ★ Don't expect to look in one place for an answer; scan the text and piece together information.

a) Put True (T), False (F), or Doesn't Say (DS) after each statement.

i) The lady has long hair. `T`

ii) She is near the table. `T`

iii) She is wearing the most impressive dress in the room. `T`

iv) She is wearing gloves and holding flowers. `T`

v) She is wearing two white shoes. `F`

vi) She is ready to go out. `DS`

vii) Pip thinks the lady is confused. `DS`

vii) The scene makes a deep impression on Pip. `?`

ix) Pip's attention is focused on the valuable jewels. `DS`

10 Read the next part of the story, in which Pip continues to describe his impressions.

It was not in the first moments that I saw all these things, though I saw more of them in the first moments than might be supposed. But I saw that everything within my view which ought to be white, had been white long ago, and had lost its lustre, and was faded and yellow. I saw that the bride within the bridal dress had withered like the dress, and like the flowers, and had no brightness left but the brightness of her sunken eyes. I saw that the dress had been put upon the rounded figure of a young woman, and that the figure upon which it now hung loose, had shrunk to skin and bone. Once, I had been taken to see some ghastly waxworks at the Fair, representing I know not what impossible personage lying in state. Once, I had been taken to one of our old marsh churches to see a skeleton in the ashes of a rich dress, that had been dug out of a vault under the church pavement. Now, waxwork and skeleton seemed to have dark eyes that moved and looked at me. I should have cried out, if I could.

Great Expectations by Charles Dickens

Now complete this summary of Pip's first impression. Choose from the words below to fill the gaps.

Pip realises that he is looking at things that had been changed by the passage of a) `time`. He realises that the lady is wearing a bridal b) `dress` that was once c) `white` but is now faded and d) `yellow`. He also understands that when the lady had first worn the dress she was younger and had a e) `plumper` figure, but now she has become thin and old. She has 'withered' and decayed, just like the dress and f) `flowers`.

| dress | time | plumper | red | thinner | yellow | flowers | white | seconds |

13

Understanding what the writer 'suggests'

Level 5 readers can understand the writer's meanings and explain them in their own words.

Level 6 readers can find deeper meanings in the text and begin to explain them using details to support their answers.

1 Read this story, set in Ancient China. It is about Haoyou, a 12-year-old boy whose father has recently died.

When Haoyou woke, he tried to move so fast that his dream could not cling to him. He determined to shake it off by the sheer speed with which he scuttled out of bed, fetched in the water, brought it to the boil. He concentrated entirely on pouring the hot water into the two cups, without spilling a drop, sprinkling the tea leaves in exactly equal numbers on to the steaming liquid. He spaced two of the cups in the precise centre of the tray, and carried it so carefully that not a single drop spilled. Then he circled the partition to where his parents' bed lay beneath a grey-morning window.

'Good morning, honoured mother and father,' he said, as he had said a thousand times.

Then the tray fell from his hands with a crash, and he stood staring at the shards* of pottery, the spreading puddle of tea. He had been trying so hard to bury his dream under everyday routine that everyday routine had undone him. This was the day after his father's funeral, and he had forgotten his father was dead. 'I'm sorry! I'm sorry! I didn't mean to say it! I forgot! No! I mean I didn't forget. Of course I didn't forget, but . . . .'

His mother sat up, still wearing the clothes of the previous day. It was plain she had not slept. She held out her arms and Haoyou ran to her, like a boat running for harbour in a storm.

shards – broken pieces

The Kite Rider by Geraldine McCaughrean

Look at the text highlighted in yellow. Read this Level 5 answer to the question:
How do you know that Haoyou's dream was unpleasant?

It says he moved 'so fast that his dream could not cling to him'.

X a) Does the answer choose the right quotations?   Yes ☐   No ☑

X b) Does the answer explain how you can tell that
       Hayou's dream was unpleasant?   Yes ☑   No ☐

Tick for work 😊 or 😐 or 😟

14

> **TIP**
> ★ Level 6 answers expect you to explain your thinking using short quotations to support your opinions.

Here's a better answer.

You know the dream was nasty because he wanted to get away from it quickly. That's why he moved 'fast'. Also that meant he could shake it off because he didn't want it to 'cling' to him. He wanted to escape from it.

explanation →

quotation →

quotation →

← explanation

2   Look at the text highlighted in blue on page 14. Plan an answer to this question:
    Explain what you learn about Haoyou's character from the way he makes the tea.

a)   Choose two quotations that contain **only** the important words.

   He (concentrated entirely) on pouring the
   water in the two cups, without spilling
   a drop) sprinkling

b)   Consider what they show you about Haoyou.

   He is really careful

c)   Write up your answer as a paragraph.

3   Look at the text highlighted in green on page 14.
    What do you learn about the feelings of Haoyou's mother from this section?

a)   Write a paragraph using the method in question 2 as a guideline.

b)   Using a highlighter, identify the quotations you used in one colour and the explanations in another colour.

c)   Check whether you are 'telling the story'. If so, add another colour.

   the
   tea
   leave
   in et

   No!

> **TIP**
> ★ Telling the story means just repeating the information in the text. Learn to spot 'telling the story' and remove it from your answers.

He concentrated entirely on pouring the hot
water into the two cups, without spilling the drops.
Sprinkling the tea leaves in exactly equal number
onto the steaming liquid. He is really careful.

15

Writers often leave things to the reader's imagination, but give **clues** to help.

4 Read the opening scene from a TV series about the Ashton family. Then add the missing stage directions from the list A to F below.

Look for clues in the text, e.g.: 'What are you doing for tea?' Donna must be coming into the kitchen to know that her mother is cooking, so the missing stage direction is **C.**

Mum:	Is that you, Donna?
Donna:	(*shouting from the hall*) No, it's the local nutter.
Mum:	How often have I told you not to slam the door? You'll break the glass one day.
Donna:	C Sorry! What are you doing for tea?
Mum:	Beans on toast.
Donna:	B Not again!
Mum:	If you want something different, cook it yourself. I've been at work all day, you know.
Donna:	A No time. Got all this homework to do.
Mum:	Clear that lot out of the way. We need somewhere to eat.
Donna:	Can't I have mine in front of the TV?
Mum:	We eat at the table in this house.
Donna:	E But look it's time for my favourite programme.
Mum:	So what? Get those things off there – now!
Donna:	F Okay, I'm going to my room. Going to get started on my work right now.
Mum:	What about your tea?
Donna:	D Not hungry!
Mum:	What have I told you about slamming doors!

A *Throwing her school bag on the table.* _____

B *Pulls a face.* _____

C *Entering the kitchen.* _____

D *Slams kitchen door on the way out.* _____

E *Pointing at the clock.* _____

F *Picking up her bag.* _____

5 Add an adverb to each stage direction in the list above to show even more understanding of the characters' moods, e.g.: **C** *Hurriedly* entering the kitchen.

6 Read the next scene, then explain how clues in a text help you to form opinions about characters.

> **TIP**
> ★ 'Explain' does not mean 'tell the story'. It means make points to answer the question using short quotations from the text.

Donna's bedroom. *She flops on the bed, and makes a call on her mobile to her friend Nadia. Switch to split screen so both Donna's and Nadia's faces are visible throughout the call.*

Nadia: Hi, Donna, how's things?

Donna: Same as usual. Mum's in a mood and she takes it out on me. I'd hardly got in the door before she started on at me.

Nadia: What about? The usual …?

Donna: No. Makes a change, doesn't it? I don't care if she doesn't like Neil. He's my boyfriend, not hers. No, this time she just blew her top when I said I wanted to have my dinner in front of the TV. She's so moody at the moment.

Nadia: Perhaps she's got something on her mind.

Donna: Yeah, making my life a misery.

Nadia: Well … I was thinking that she might be missing your dad.

Donna: What's that got to do with her making my life a misery? They never got on when they were together.

Nadia: What I mean is that she might be under pressure … you know, being a single mum now – money worries, that sort of thing. Missing him in that way.

Donna: If anyone is missing him, it's me. She didn't think about me when she told him to get out, did she?

Nadia: Hmm … well, look, Donna, do you want to come round here for a bit? Might take the pressure off both of you. I can help you out with that maths assignment. I know you've been putting off doing it. Come on, we'll get it done in no time.

Donna: What do you mean putting it off?

Nadia: Just trying to …

Donna: Well don't. I can look after myself, thanks very much.

Donna ends the call and Nadia's face fades from the screen.

7 What impression do you get of Nadia and Donna? Use examples from the script to support your answer.

Nadia is kind and helpful. I know this because in the text it mentions that she wants to help out Donna with her maths assignment. Donna is short-tempered. This is because in the text it says that she can take care of herself.

17

Level 6 readers can find deeper meanings in the text and begin to explain them using details to support their answers.

Level 7 readers can interpret meanings from what is said and what is unsaid in a text.

Sometimes you will need to consider a range of 'clues' to understand characters or themes in a text.

8 Read this text. It comes from a story set in the 1890s about the fictional detective Sherlock Holmes. A client seeking help has arrived …

A lady dressed in black and heavily veiled, who had been sitting in the window, rose as we entered.

'Good morning, madam,' said Holmes cheerily. 'My name is Sherlock Holmes. This is my intimate friend and associate, Doctor Watson, before whom you can speak as freely as before myself. Ha, I am glad to see that Mrs Hudson has had the good sense to light the fire. Pray draw up to it, and I shall order you a cup of hot coffee, for I observe that you are shivering.'

The Speckled Band by Sir Arthur Conan Doyle

a) Highlight any words or phrases in the text that you think might be useful in preparing an answer to the question:

   What evidence is there in this extract to suggest that Holmes can be a thoughtful host?

b) Next, read this answer and check whether it includes all the information you found. Highlight each piece of evidence in the answer.

Holmes shows he's thoughtful because he's welcoming and cheerful when he meets the lady. He explains who Doctor Watson is to put the lady at ease and so she can feel free to talk. He's also very considerate because he thinks the woman is 'shivering' with cold and suggests she move nearer to the fire. He offers her 'hot coffee' to make her more comfortable.

Extending your answers using a main point and discussion of evidence will help you develop your skills for GCSE English.

Here's a strategy for writing longer answers.

★ Highlight helpful evidence in the text.

★ Consider what it suggests to you.

★ Check if there is more than one possible interpretation. If so, mention both in your answer.

Write up your ideas in one or two paragraphs, including quotations.

9 Now read the next part of the text and practise writing an extended answer.

'It is not cold which makes me shiver,' said the woman in a low voice, changing her seat as requested.

'What then?'

'It is fear, Mr Holmes. It is terror.' She raised her veil as she spoke, and we could see that she was indeed in a pitiable state of agitation, her face all drawn and grey, with restless, frightened eyes, like those of some hunted animal. Her features and figure were those of a woman of thirty, but her hair was shot with premature grey, and her expression was weary and haggard. Sherlock Holmes ran her over with one of his quick, all-comprehensive glances.

'You must not fear,' said he soothingly, bending forward and patting her forearm. We shall soon set matters right, I have no doubt. You have come in by train this morning, I see.'

'You know me, then?'

'No, but I observe the second half of a return ticket in the palm of your left glove …'

The Speckled Band by Sir Arthur Conan Doyle

What impression do you get of Sherlock Holmes during this conversation? Refer closely to the text to support your answer.   (3 marks)

I know that he's a detective ∝ because he found out the lady went on a train that morning.

_____

_____

_____

_____

When you have completed your answer, compare it with the one in the answer section on page 46.

TIP ★ Practise writing answers to questions that need a longer response.

Writers use the power of suggestion to give layers of meaning to a text. At Level 7, you need to show that you can understand those layers of meaning. To do this you will need to refer to well-chosen quotations.

10 Read this text. The writer is planning a camping trip in an area where black bears live. His preparation includes reading a book about bear attacks.

> I won't say I became obsessed by all this, but it did occupy my thoughts a great deal in the months while I waited for the spring to come. My particular dread – the vivid possibility that left me staring at tree shadows on the bedroom ceiling night after night – was having to lie in a small tent, alone in an inky wilderness, listening to a foraging bear outside, and wondering what its intentions were. I was especially riveted by a photograph taken late at night by a camper with a flash at a campground out west. The photograph caught four black bears as they puzzled over a suspended food bag. The bears were clearly startled but not remotely alarmed by the flash. It was not the size or demeanour of the bears that troubled me – they looked almost comically un-aggressive, like four guys who had got a Frisbee caught up a tree – but their numbers. Up to that moment it had not occurred to me that bears might prowl in parties. What on earth would I do if four bears came into my camp?
>
> *A Walk in the Woods* by Bill Bryson

> **TIP** ★ Read the text to get a general idea of what it is about. Then search for the information you need.

a) Answer this question to practise identifying the right quotation to support an opinion:
   Quote the word the writer uses to suggest the complete darkness of Bill's imagined forest.

b) Here are four answers given by pupils, along with the teacher's comments. Draw lines to match the answers to the comments.

Pupil answers	Teacher comments
A 'shadows'	i Describes bears, not the forest.
B 'inky'	ii Refers to a time, not a forest.
C 'black'	iii Describes what Bill Bryson really saw on his bedroom ceiling.
D 'night'	iv Suggests blackness and linked to imaginary forest.

If you made the correct matches, then you have shown you can read the question carefully.

> **TIP**
>
> ★ Some questions look easy because they just ask for one word, but take care! Scan through the text to check out possible answers. (The first thing you find isn't always the right answer!)

11 Next, consider a question that asks you to explain how a writer suggests a meaning:
Explain how the writer suggests that his fear of the black bears was so strong that it prevented him from sleeping.
Refer to the text to support your answer.   (3 marks)

Here's a thoughtful student's collection of ideas.

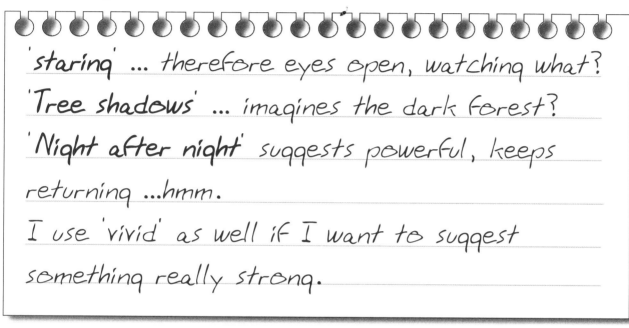

'staring' ... therefore eyes open, watching what?

'Tree shadows' ... imagines the dark forest?

'Night after night' suggests powerful, keeps returning ...hmm.

I use 'vivid' as well if I want to suggest something really strong.

Use the ideas to help you write your own answer.

_____

_____

_____

_____

_____

_____

_____

_____

_____

_____

Commenting on text organisation

Level 5 readers can identify the pattern of ideas in a text and make comments about it.
Level 6 readers can understand the reason why a writer places ideas in a particular order.

Look at this argument about school uniform. You will see that the writer uses a FOR + AGAINST + FOR organisation. Ending on a positive note is one way to persuade a reader that the writer is right.

School uniform is the same for everyone, which is fair.	However, it doesn't give pupils much freedom of expression.	Overall, it is usually a practical style that lets everyone focus on their work.
FOR	AGAINST	FOR

1   Read this web page from the charity Oxfam. Then highlight the topic sentences.

http://www.oxfam.org.uk/donate/yourmoney.html

How we spend your money

You're only a few clicks away from providing the support that could change someone's life. It's amazing how much can be achieved with just a small amount of money from people like you and a little help from Oxfam.

Giving regularly really is the best way to support Oxfam. It means we have reliable income we can count on which allows us to plan in advance and budget more effectively.

What can you buy for 16p a day? You might think 'not much these days' but a gift of 16p a day (that's just £5 per month), can provide basic essentials like clean water and healthcare, and life-changing opportunities like education and small-business training to the people who need them most.

For every £1 you give to Oxfam

80p is spent directly on emergency, development and campaigning work

10p is spent on support and running costs

10p is invested to generate future income

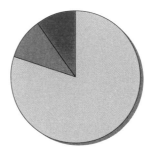

TIP ★ Topic sentences will help you to identify ideas.

At Level 6, readers are expected to identify the reason **why** a writer puts ideas in a particular order, e.g.:

Level 5 part of answer

The writer begins the third paragraph with a question to challenge the reader rather than just giving facts.

Level 6 part of answer

2 How does the writer organise the text to have an impact on the reader?
Read these comments and mark them as Level 5 or Level 6. Then highlight the part of the response that makes it a Level 6 answer.

a)

Paragraphs 1 and 4 are both about how little money is needed to make a difference.

b)

Paragraph 3 gives general examples of how money can help. Paragraph 4 then gives precise information about how money is spent to show the reader that every penny counts.

c)

The writer refers to money in paragraphs 3 and 4, and gives examples of how money is spent.

d)

The first and last paragraphs are linked because they show readers that even a little makes a difference. The writer uses the first section to open up the idea and the last section to prove it.

3 In the bullet points, why has the writer presented the figures in this order?

_____

_____

_____

TIP ★ Identify any link between the beginning and ending of a story. Then try to work out how the other sections fit together.

4 Read this text. It is the beginning of a story set in China about a young girl called Lu Si-yan.

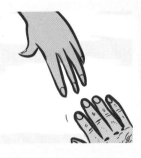

I loved my baby brother, until Uncle took me to market and sold me. He was the bright, shiny pebble in the water, the twinkling star in the sky. Until Uncle took me to market and sold me. Then I hated him.

'Lu Si-yan,' Uncle greeted me early one summer morning, 'today is a big day for you. From today, you must learn to find your own way in the muddy whirlpool of life. Your mother and I have given you a good start. Now it is your turn.' [C] [D]

My mother stood in the shadows of our kitchen, but she didn't look at me and she didn't say a word. Uncle took me tightly by the wrist. As he led me from the house, my mother reached out her hand towards me and clawed the air as though trying to pull me back. Then she picked up my little brother and hid behind the door, but I saw her face wither with pain and, in that moment, fear gripped my heart. [B C] [A]

'Where are you taking me, Uncle Ba?' I cried.

Spilled Water by Sally Grindley, Bloomsbury

a) Underline the most shocking phrase in the first paragraph.

b) How does this link with the last sentence? It has the same subject.

c) Why has the writer given away such important information in the first paragraph?

this is the introduction.

TIP ★ A one-sentence summary of the 'job' of each section can help you to see a pattern in the text.

5 Use comments A–D to label paragraphs 2 and 3. Use the boxes beside the text.

A The mother knows a terrible thing is about to happen.

B The reader knows the girl is about to be tricked.

C The writer shows the girl's emotions.

D The uncle makes it sound like a good thing is going to happen

6 How does knowing that Lu Si-yan is going to be sold affect how you read the other paragraphs?

this is because this has the most main shocking problem.

> ★ Identify the 'job' of each section. Then consider why the writer put the sections in this order.

7 Read the opening of this novel about a boy in the 1800s who wants to be a sailor.

One night at supper I told my father I wanted to become a sailor. He laughed at first, not taking me seriously. But when I insisted, his face grew darker.

'The Navy's a brutal calling, Sam, only suitable for brutal men. You're a thinker, you're a sensitive boy, and you're still young, for heaven's sake. I'll not have you waste your talents with the thugs and sweepings of our gaols that fill the Navy ships.' Then his voice softened. 'Besides – I want to see you grow up and marry. I want you to look after your mother and me in our old age! We don't want you getting yourself killed hundreds of miles away from home.'

My mother stayed silent, but her eyes filled with tears. There had been four of us boys once, rather than two. Smallpox carried off my two younger brothers when I was six. Now there was just my older brother Thomas and me. He was more of a timid soul and not so interested in the world. It was Tom who would inherit my father's shop.

My father had in mind that I would teach at the village school and help my uncle run his shop. A life selling groceries would suit Tom fine.

But not me. I always wanted to escape from the vast, flat horizon of Norfolk, with only the flapping sails of a few creaking windmills to break the silence. Grey and grim it is for two-thirds of the year, with a biting wind coming straight off the North Sea. Reverend Chatham, our village parson, says there are barely three hundred people in the parish. Imagine just seeing those same few faces for the rest of your life?

Powder Monkey by Paul Dowswell, Bloomsbury

What is the 'job' of each section? Write your answer alongside each paragraph.

8 How does the order of the information in the opening of this story help to keep the reader interested?

> ★ There may not be one correct answer to the practice question. You have to show that **you** can make connections and **explain** them to a teacher or examiner.

Level 6 readers can identify and comment on how texts are organised.
Level 7 readers can evaluate the effect of some features of text organisation.

Some texts are organised using a 'pattern'. If you can find this pattern, you can think about **why** it is used and whether it is **effective**.

9   Read this story about a girl, Kate, who changes into a wolf – and enjoys it. This section describes the build-up to the change.

(It's) late. The moon, full and fat, is blindingly bright through the window above Kate Folan's bed. It's not a comforting light. It only makes the wide night sky seem even blacker.

emotion   *possession*

Kate can feel it through the glass, bathing her sweating skin like iced water.

She's so hot.

She leans over and heaves open the window. Her shaky breath mists out and mingles with the humid night air. She lifts the damp dark hair from the back of her neck, to expose it to the cool breeze.

So many scents and sounds carry in from outside (...) *ellipses*

There's a tiny electric buzz sparking in her bones. It tickles and warms her, as if her whole body is itching on the inside and she has no way to scratch. It's maddening. Dizzying.

The Wereling: Wounded by Stephen Cole, Bloomsbury

a) Use the list in the table to identify any features in this story. Circle the evidence in the story and label it.

b) Think about the effect of the feature on the rest of the text and complete the table below.

Features	What is the effect on the text?
Long sentences	Hooks the reader
Short sentences	Creates more suspence
Single word sentences	Makes the reader read on
Lists	giving more description about setting and character
Short paragraphs	Show the main action in small pieces which focuses more attention onto each part – creating a jerky effect … maybe to show how the change feels to Kate.

> TIP ★ Evaluating **why** the organisational features are used and whether they are effective is important for Level 7.

10 Read the story as it continues.

Kate shuts her eyes, shakes her head. She wants to let go. To lose the fear and the doubts — just give in to the craving. Why should she fight it? This has to happen …

Kate's heart begins to pound. It feels like a fist knocking against her ribs, so hard it hurts. She can see its movement beneath the soaked white cotton of her night-clothes.

The moon seems incandescent, like it has caught fire.

Kate knows now. It will happen tonight. The burning heat now pounding through her body seems to be melting her bones. The pain is delicious, irresistible. Kate wonders how she could ever have wished it away.

The change feels maddeningly near now. Why won't it come?

The Wereling: Wounded by Stephen Cole, Bloomsbury

These statements are all pupil responses to the question: *How does the writer organise this text to build up tension?* Are they correct (C) or incorrect (I)?

a) The writer generally uses short paragraphs with short sentences to give a quick rhythm to the text, like her heart beat. ☐ C

_____

_____

_____

b) Two questions are used. Not because they need an answer, but to show the reader that Kate is willing for this to happen, which goes against the expected reaction where people don't want to be werewolves. ☐ I

_____

_____

_____

c) A single-sentence paragraph about the moon is the only sentence not directly about Kate. It stands alone to remind the reader that something else controls the change, not her. ☐ I

_____

_____

_____

11 Read this article about a Formula 1 car race in Monaco, focusing on Lewis Hamilton, a British driver.

FORMULA 1

Sunday 1 June 2008

Lewis Hamilton is not stupid enough to believe that his dramatic win in Monaco last Sunday means that he will triumph again next week. His drive, in the trickiest conditions imaginable, was world class, but Hamilton will be the first to accept that luck played a major part. He will also be aware that another car would probably have won this race had all things been equal. Fortunately for Hamilton, things are rarely equal at Monaco. Particularly when it rains.

A light shower, mixed with the oil and grime always found on a public road, produced a surface so slippery that it went beyond the capability of his excellent wet weather tyres and Hamilton's sublime skill. A brush with the crash barrier on lap six actually did him a favour and accidentally knocked Hamilton on to a strategy that would turn out to be perfect.

In this article, the writer makes a number of connections between the two paragraphs.

a) Spot the connections and explain how they work. Use the table below for your answers. An example has been done for you.

Evidence		Explanation
Paragraph 1	**Paragraph 2**	
not stupid	sublime skill	Builds up respect for Hamilton by repeating a reference to his skill or intelligence.
the trickiest conditions		
luck		
Fortunately for Hamilton		
when it rains		

b) Write your answer to the question:
   How does the writer organise the text to show the reader that Lewis Hamilton had a difficult race?

_____

_____

_____

_____

_____

_____

_____

_____

_____

_____

_____

Commenting on the writer's use of language

> Level 5 readers can identify interesting language effects and make short comments about them.
> **Level 6 readers can give more detailed comments on a writer's use of language.**

TIP
★ Read a text once to find out what happens.
Then read it again to identify interesting language.

1 This story was written in 1860. It is about an orphan boy, Pip. It begins with him crying at the family tombstone. But suddenly, he is not alone … Read it twice and make a note of any interesting language.

'Hold your noise!' cried a terrible voice, as a man started up from among the graves at the side of the church porch. 'Keep still, you little devil, or I'll cut your throat!'

A fearful man, all in coarse grey, with a great iron on his leg. A man with no hat, and with broken shoes, and with an old rag tied round his head. A man who had been soaked in water, and smothered in mud, and lamed by stones, and cut by flints, and stung by nettles, and torn by briars; who limped, and shivered, and glared and growled; and whose teeth chattered in his head as he seized me by the chin.

'O! Don't cut my throat, sir,' I pleaded in terror. 'Pray don't do it, sir.'

Great Expectations by Charles Dickens

a) Using different coloured highlighters, find examples in the text of:
   ★ repetition – a word or phrase repeated several times;
   ★ a list – it can be a list of words or phrases;
   ★ alliteration – words beginning with the same letter or sound.

b) How do these language effects help to make the man seem frightening?

c) Read this sample Level 5 answer to part b).

'Glared and growled' help to make the man seem frightening and maybe a bit like an animal.

Circle the quotation in this answer.

d) Now write an answer to explain the use of repetition and the list.

TIP

★ At Level 6, readers may pick the same quotations as at Level 5, but their comments are more detailed.

2 Read this text about a man, Victor Frankenstein, who creates a creature made from parts of other bodies. This is the moment the creature comes to life.

phrase to suggest dull light

It was on a dreary night of November that I beheld the accomplishment of my toils. With an anxiety that almost amounted to agony, I collected the instruments of life around me, that I might infuse a spark of being into the lifeless thing that lay at my feet. It was already one in the morning; the rain pattered dismally against the panes, and my candle was nearly burnt out, when, by the glimmer of the half-extinguished light, I saw the dull yellow eye of the creature open; it breathed hard, and a convulsive motion agitated its limbs.

Frankenstein by Mary Shelley

a) How does the writer use language to create a miserable setting?
Highlight all the words or phrases linked to light or colour. Write a few sentences about the words as in the example below, commenting in detail on at least two words or phrases.

> The writer makes the scene seem miserable by referring to dull light. It is 'dreary', which sounds dull and heavy, and darkness is suggested by 'night' and 'November'.

explanations linking quotations and question   **short quotations**

b) Choose two more words or phrases from the text to comment on in detail. Write a few sentences about the words as in the example above.

c) Underline three short explanations in your answer.

d) Now check your work. Do your comments:

★ link to the question?   **YES** or **NO**

★ use short supporting quotations?   **YES** or **NO**

31

Writers sometimes use **contrast** to make an impression with language.

> **TIP**
> ★ A 'contrast' is like a 'difference'. When things are different from each other, you notice them more sharply.

3 Read this story, in which the writer presents the farmer as an unpleasant man right from the start.

> Mr Jones, of the Manor Farm, had locked the hen-houses for the night, but was too drunk to remember to shut the pop-holes. With the ring of light from his lantern dancing from side to side, he lurched across the yard, kicked off his boots at the back door, drew himself a last glass of beer from the barrel in the scullery, and made his way up to bed, where Mrs Jones was already snoring.
>
> As soon as the light in the bedroom went out there was a stirring and a fluttering all through the farm buildings. Word had gone round during the day that old Major, the prize Middle White boar, had had a strange dream on the previous night and wished to communicate it to the other animals. It had been agreed that they should all meet in the big barn as soon as Mr Jones was safely out of the way.

Animal Farm by George Orwell

Complete this commentary on the language in the story by using the words in the box below to fill the gaps.

The words and phrases highlighted in a) _____ describe how

Mr Jones moves. Those highlighted in b) _____ describe the

movements of other things. The fact that everything except Mr Jones moves

in a c) _____ and d) _____ way makes him seem even

e) _____ and f) _____ .

| clumsier | yellow | interesting | slower | green | light |

4 Read this article, in which the writer 'plays' with language to make a serious article sound more fun.

How to invest in collectible toys

If you're clearing out the attic and just about to throw away your childhood toys, think again. They may be worth more than just sentimental value.

The magnetic pull of a toyshop is a standard childhood memory. And an early passion for Lego, Action Man or Barbie never quite fades. So it is not surprising that collectible toys are a prime investment, with select examples realising very grown-up prices at auction.

A white Steiff teddy bear from 1925, for example, fetched £25,200 – more than five times the estimate – at an auction house in 2006.

David Nathan of Vectis Toy Auctions says that older items – typically pre-1970s – are the safest bet, provided they are in mint condition and boxed. 'Some new toys will rocket in price; most won't. It is hard to make that call. With older items, you know whether or not there is a market. Even so, trends come and go. Antique dolls are weak at the moment, while teddies are strong, for example.'

He adds: 'One definite no-no should be all new limited-edition toys. Buyers almost always keep them in cabinets or whatever, so a perfect example is nothing rare. In contrast, 99 per cent of ordinary toys get play-worn, which means the boxed ones are special.'

> **TIP**
> ★ Word opposites can also build up a pattern for the writer to use, e.g. toys – serious stuff.

a) First, read the text. Then read again and highlight any words linked to toys or children that may be used to make the article sound more fun.

b) Explain how these words or phrases add humour to a serious business article.

> **TIP**
> ★ Remember: QUOTATION + EXPLANATION

Level 6 readers can comment in some detail on a writer's choice of language.
Level 7 readers can analyse the writer's language for its effect.

5   In this story, the narrator first speaks to the reader to explain his state of mind.

Punctuation used to show hesitation and anxiety.

> True! – nervous – very, very dreadfully nervous I had been and am! But why will you say that I am mad? The disease had sharpened my senses – not destroyed – not dulled them. Above all was the sense of hearing acute. I heard all things in the heaven and in the earth. I heard many things in hell. How, then, am I mad? Hearken! and observe how healthily – how calmly I can tell you the whole story.
>
> *The Tell-Tale Heart* by Edgar Allen Poe

a) Warm up your language analysis skills by identifying which language features have been used in this text. Explain the effect of the features by labelling the boxes.

b) Give one effect of each language feature.

TIP
★ Make sure you explain your analysis well, building quotations into your sentences. Comment on language, not just content.

c) Read the pupil answer below to the question:
    How does the writer use language to show that the man is mad?

There are **three** points in this answer. Use different coloured highlighters to check that they have all been analysed thoroughly. Identify **Point**, **Explanation**, **Evidence** for each point made. One example has been done for you.

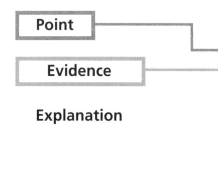

Point

Evidence

Explanation

The writer wants the reader to understand that the narrator is mad, even though the narrator denies this. In fact, the repeated 'mad?' almost guarantees that he is mad. The madness also comes through in the language. For example, dashes are used to break up sentences and make it seem that the speaker is anxious or can't keep his thoughts together. Referring to 'heaven' and 'hell' and 'hearing' things also suggest the ideas of voices in the head that insane people sometimes experience.

TIP

★ We all know when we enjoy a text. Maybe it's terrifying, sad or really funny. But Level 7 readers will ask themselves: *How* did it make me feel this way? and *Why* did it work? Level 7 readers can analyse how a text works.

6 Read this text. It is the story of a girl who has been transformed into a fox for the first time.

Somehow she had become something else. Yet there was no sense that this experience was in any way unreal, indeed nothing had ever seemed more real. She breathed deeply. This was no dream. The lightest of breezes frilled the thick hairs of her winter coat. The sensation was pleasurable and quite unlike anything else she'd ever felt. She had not always been like this. She had not always had this dark red fur. It was all wrong. She struggled to remember what she had been expecting. She had not been expecting this. She could smell the moist mustiness of the fermenting leaves, the loam of a fecund earth. Even in the darkness each variation in texture in the tree bark and each small gradation of colour in the fallen leaves was acutely visible as if she viewed everything through a portable microscope. This was beyond her imagination. She should have had hands, that was it, she should have had hands and so how could she have a paw where a hand should be?

Hunted by N.M. Browne, Bloomsbury

a) *How does the writer use language to make the girl changing into a fox seem real to the reader?*

(5 marks)

b) Highlight any language features you think may help you to answer the question.

c) Double-check that these features are relevant.

7 a) Write up your analysis using the Point, Explanation, Evidence approach practised on page 34. Your opening phrase could be:

The writer makes this strange experience seem real by ...

b) Check your work with highlighter pens to identify points, explanations and evidence.

There are language patterns in non-fiction texts as well as in fiction, but the purposes may be different. However, you can use the same technique to identify and analyse them.

1. Read to understand – and enjoy.

2. Look out for interesting words and phrases. (Use a highlighter.)

3. Analyse how those words and phrases help the writer to achieve an effect – humour, suspense, authority, etc.

8   Read this text about Eddie Edwards, the first British Olympic ski jumper.

Eddie the Eagle lives on

The adoring public will love you for trying your best despite having no skill, fitness or technique. Even though you may be the subject of endless jokes in the media, you are remembered more than the winners. After all, can you name the winners of the 1988 Olympic ski jumping? No. But I'll bet you know who came last.

Eddie 'The Eagle' Edwards made history as Britain's first ever ski jumper at the Winter Olympics, in 1988. He finished a glorious last in both of the distances he attempted, but won the heart of the public.

If you think it is just the winners that count, think again. They may get the money, medals and advertising contracts. But, if you are a real loser, the reward can be even greater – immortality.

a) How does the writer use language to make this article amusing for the reader?

b) Choose two of the highlighted examples and explain how they might help to amuse the reader.

> **TIP**
> ★ Imagine the writer reading aloud to help you understand their tone of voice and how the language helps to deliver this.

9 Read this article about white-water rafting. The writer chooses language to make the experience seem both funny and exciting by careful use of words and phrases.

River crew ... full steam ahead on the mighty Franklin.

Style? Nil points. I'm sopping wet, clinging to the seat of an inflatable raft, facing the wrong way up a thunderous wall of water. Just before my oversize helmet slips across my eyes delivering temporary blindness, I catch sight of a warning panel: 'Do not exceed your paddling ability. Be honest with yourself.'

OK, I will. I'm out of my depth. But who cares? This is a heady shot of adrenaline – a high voltage jolt for a lethargic city soul. And it's not as if I'm alone. I'm in the secure, sun-scorched hands of two bush-savvy local guides.

They're as essential as life jackets and helmets if you take on the Franklin, one of the savage rivers that riddle south-west Tasmania like a nest of snakes. Their knowledge and experience turn a potentially lethal expedition into a glorious mix of exertion, excitement and silent contemplation.

a) Use the three steps on page 36 to plan how to answer this question:
   How does the writer use language to make the experience seem both funny and exciting?

b) Write your answer in a few paragraphs.

Commenting on the writer's viewpoint and purpose

> Level 5 readers can identify the purpose of a text and begin to explain the effect of the text on the reader.
>
> **Level 6 readers can explain how the writer achieves a purpose, using quotations and references from the text.**

1 Read this autobiographical text by Roald Dahl. He recalls pretending to be ill, so he could be sent home from boarding school (which he hated). He is talking to the family doctor who is a friend of his mother's.

> He sat himself down behind his desk and fixed me with a penetrating but not unkindly eye. 'You're faking, aren't you?' he said.
>
> 'How do you know?' I blurted out.
>
> 'Because your stomach is soft and perfectly normal,' he answered. 'If you had had an inflammation down there, the stomach would have been hard and rigid. It's quite easy to tell.'
>
> I kept silent.
>
> 'I expect you're homesick,' he said.
>
> I nodded miserably.
>
> 'Everyone is at first,' he said. 'You have to stick it out. And don't blame your mother for sending you away to boarding school. She insisted you were too young to go, but it was I who persuaded her it was the right thing to do. Life is tough, and the sooner you learn how to cope with it the better for you.'
>
> 'What will you tell the school?' I asked him, trembling.
>
> 'I'll say you had a very severe infection of the stomach which I am curing with pills,' he answered smiling. It will mean that you must stay home for three more days. But promise me you won't try anything like this again …'
>
> *Boy* by Roald Dahl

a) On a separate piece of paper, answer the practice question below.

PRACTICE QUESTION

What impressions are given about the young Roald Dahl as he sits in front of the doctor? Support you answer with references to the text.   **(3 marks)**

---

b) Now look at this pupil response. Is the answer correct or incorrect?

He's frightened because he has done something wrong and he thinks he might get into trouble.

c) Look at the descriptions of Level 5 and Level 6 readers at the top of this page. What level do you think this answer is?

The answer was OK, but does not give the whole picture and there are no references or quotations to back it up.

 ★ Take time to research a full answer.

2 Circle whether each of these statements is True or False.

a) Roald Dahl owns up almost immediately.   **True / False**

b) He's too frightened to make excuses.   **True / False**

c) He becomes sad and fearful.   **True / False**

d) He is amazed at the doctor's cleverness.   **True / False**

e) He is disappointed that his plan did not work.   **True / False**

Now check the answer page.

3 Highlight in red the sentences that helped to build up your impression. They will give you the references or quotations you need to support your answer.

If you've done this carefully, you have probably picked out these sentences:

'How do you know?' I blurted out.

I kept silent.

I nodded miserably.

'What will you tell the school?' I asked him, trembling.

 ★ It is important to scan through the whole text to form an opinion rather than just look closely at one area. This will help you to do well in questions that give 3 or 5 marks.

4 Now write a better answer to the practice question on page 38. Use a separate piece of paper.

5 Use your research skills to answer this more difficult practice question:

PRACTICE QUESTION

What different impressions does the reader get about the doctor in this text? Support your answer with references from the text.

(3 marks)

_____

_____

_____

_____

_____

6 Read this text in which a school inspector has been asked to give advice on a particular pupil. Phinn describes what happened when he visited the school.

When the children had taken off their coats and changed into their indoor shoes, they sat at their desks ready for the register to be called. All, that is, except one child. He was a sharp-faced boy of about nine or ten with a scattering of freckles, wavy red hair and a tight little mouth which curved downwards. This, I guessed, was Terry.

The Other Side of the Dale by Gervase Phinn

The writer's purpose is to focus on one pupil. Complete this explanation of how the writer does this. Choose words from the words in the box to fill the gaps.

The writer sets the scene in the first sentence but then zooms in on one particular pupil in the sentence, 'All, that is, except one child.' That sentence is a) **short** and snappy so it focuses attention on that child.

Next, the writer b) **describes** that particular child in some detail.

That makes the child more c) **real** for the reader. Then, the d) **last** sentence tells us the child's name. It sticks in the mind even more because it is the final e) **impression** given in the paragraph.

| describes | short | last | impression | real |

TIP ★ A writer can have more than one purpose!

7 a) Is it a positive or negative impression of Terry?

   b) Highlight words and phrases in the story that support your opinion.

   c) Write a paragraph to explain how the writer creates this impression.

The writer made a bad impression on Terry by him not going in class on time. He also has a bad, scary description As they guessed, It was a boy called Terry, he must be bad behaved.

8 Read the next part of the story and see whether you were right.

'Come along, please, Terry,' said Miss Pilkington firmly, 'take your seat.'

'Who's he, then?' asked the child, pointing in my direction.

'That's Mr Phinn, and please don't point, it's rude.'

'Is he a copper?'

'Just take a seat will you, please, Terry,' said the teacher.

'He looks like a copper. Are you a copper?'

'Terry, will you take a seat,' repeated the teacher firmly.

'I can smell coppers a mile off.' The child slumped into a chair. 'He's either a copper or a probation officer.'

'And take what you are chewing out of your mouth, please, Terry,' said Miss Pilkington.

'Haven't finished it yet.' He looked back at me. 'I bet he is a copper.'

'Put what you are chewing in here, please Terry,' said the teacher firmly, holding up a waste-paper basket.

The boy ambled to the front and dropped a bullet of chewing gum in the bin.

The Other Side of the Dale by Gervase Phinn

Two people are now in focus: Miss Pilkington and Terry.

Try this practice question about these characters.

PRACTICE QUESTION

What impressions are you given of Terry and Miss Pilkington? You should consider:

★ what Terry says;

★ what he does;

★ how Miss Pilkington talks.

Support your answer with brief quotations from the text.

(3 marks)

Terry doesn't listen to the teacher as in the text it says, 'Are you a copper? He looks like a copper.' This tells us that he is very lazy and he ambled to put his gum in the bin. It also tells us that Miss Pilkington is strict and snappy. I know this because in the text it says, 'Terry will you take a seat.' It also tells us she's a firm person and teacher.

TIP

★ Use your highlighter to mark out useful quotations.

41

Level 6 readers can explain how the writer achieves a purpose, using quotations and references from the text.

Level 7 readers can analyse how a writer's viewpoint and purpose are presented and developed across a text.

Texts can give the reader viewpoints in different ways.

9   Read this text, written by Ah-nen-la-de-ni, a member of the Native American Mohawk tribe in the late 19th century. Here he writes about being taken into a boarding school.

AH-NEN-LA-DE-NI

When I was thirteen a great change occurred, for the honey-tongued agent of a new Government contract school appeared on the reservation, drumming up boys and girls for his institution. He made a great impression by going from house to house and describing, through an interpreter, all the glories and luxuries of the new place, the good food and teaching, the fine uniforms, the playground and its sports and toys. All that a wild boy had to do, according to the agent, was to attend this school for a year or two, and he was sure to emerge with all the knowledge and skill of the white man.

An Indian Boy's Story by Ah-nen-la-de-ni

Investigate how the text influences the reader into taking different viewpoints.

a) First, consider this question:
    What kind of impression did the agent create about the school and the results it could achieve?
    Refer to the text to support your answer.

b) Next, with coloured pens, highlight words and phrases in the text that:
    i)   present an attractive view of the school;
    ii) show what results the school could achieve.

10 Read this pupil's response to question 10a on page 42. Then answer Yes (Y) or No (N) to the questions below.

> He made the school sound amazing. He said it had 'luxuries' and that pupils would be well fed there and given 'fine clothes' and toys. They would also have good teachers, a playground and sports facilities. He said if they went there, they would come out knowing as much as a white person and be as skillful.

Has the pupil:

a) answered both parts of the question?   Y

b) used relevant quotations to support their opinion?   Y

c) explained relevant parts of the text in his own words?   Y

If you put 'Yes' three times, you've recognised a good answer about one viewpoint in the text.

11 The writer hints in the text that he doesn't approve of the agent.

a) Underline the phrase 'honey-tongued agent' and think about why the writer has used this language.

b) Read this pupil response to the question:
Explain why the writer describes the agent as 'honey-tongued'.
Refer to the text to support your explanation.

> The writer wants to show he doesn't really trust the agent now. As he looks back and writes his life story, he thinks the agent was just sweet-talking them. He was 'honey-tongued' like he was just out to impress them. He wanted to make it as it text

12 Read the next part of the text and you'll see that the pupil had clearly understood the writer's purpose.

Next, try to provide an answer to the question:
What different impressions of the government school are given in the whole extract?
Refer to the text to support your answer.

(5 marks)

Writers can influence readers to respond in different ways.

13 Read this text. It is from a short story about a boy, Charles Manders, who is visiting a boarding school. He is taken by the headmaster's wife to meet the Lower Third, the year group he might be joining.

> 'Now this is the Lower Third, Charles, who you'd be with if you come to us in September. Boys, this is Charles Manders, and I want you to tell him all about things and answer any questions he wants to ask. You can believe about half of what they say, Charles, and they will tell you the most fearful lies about the food, which is excellent.'
>
> The boys laugh and groan; amiable, exaggerated groans. They must like the headmaster's wife; there is licensed repartee. They look at her with bright eyes in open, eager faces. Someone leaps to hold the door for her, and close it behind her. She is gone.
>
> *Next Term, We'll Mash You* by Penelope Lively

Complete these tasks to investigate how the writer of the text above influences the reader's response.

a) Consider the question:
Describe what impression is given of the school.
You should comment on:
  ★ how the head's wife talks to the boys;
  ★ how the boys react to her.
Support your answer with references and quotations from the text.

b) Read this answer and complete the teacher's comments.

> It seems a very friendly place. The head's wife is very relaxed with the boys. The boys like her and they are polite to her. The school seems to be a happy place.

You've got the main points but your answer lacks ⟨ ⟩

and ⟨ ⟩ .

c) Highlight any useful brief quotations in the text.

d) On a separate piece of paper, give an improved and more detailed answer.

14 Read how the story continues, then complete the tasks that follow, which will prepare you for question 15.

The child stands in the centre of the room, and it draws in around him. The circle of children contracts, faces are only a yard or so from him, strange faces, looking, assessing.

Asking questions. They help themselves to his name, his age, his school. Over their heads he sees beyond the window an inaccessible world of shivering trees and high racing clouds and his voice which floated like a feather in the dusty schoolroom air dies altogether and he becomes mute, and he stands in the middle of them with shoulders humped, staring down at feet: grubby plimsolls and kicked brown sandals. There is a noise in his ears like rushing water, a torrential din out of which voices boom, blotting each other out so that he cannot always hear the words. Do you? They say, and Have you? and What's your? and the faces, if he looks up, swing into one another in kaleidoscopic patterns and the floor under his feet is unsteady, lifting and falling.

And out of the noises comes one voice that is complete, that he can hear. 'Next term, we'll mash you,' it says. 'We always mash new boys.'

Next Term, We'll Mash You by Penelope Lively

a) Think of the three paragraphs as scenes in a film. How would you present them to show whose perspective they are from? For example:

Para 1: view from above as faces draw in circling around the boy

Para 2: _____

_____

Para 3: _____

_____

b) Highlight the questions at the end of paragraph 2 and think about what effect is created.

c) Think about what effect is created by the final paragraph.

15 You should now be able to tackle the question:
Explain how the reader is made to feel that being in the school room has become a threatening experience for Charles.
Use references and quotations from the text to support your answer.

Pages 6–9: Finding and using information in a text (L5–6)

1   a) False (line to 'largest tribe')
    b) False (line to 'live almost entirely')
    c) flat – False (line to 'rolling hills'), ugly – False (line to 'stunning landscape'), desert – False (line to 'lush pasture')

2   a) Mtele knew the area. The ranger was experienced and had a gun.
    b) Mears was new to area/Mears was not local/Mtele was used to the conditions.

3   protection from animals; gives light; gives heat; gives comfort; a signal for other travellers

5   Camp site C

6   a) Instruction B
    b) 1–C; 2–B; 3–E; 4–D; 5–A; 6–F

Pages 10–13: Finding and using information in a text (L6–7)

7   a) 3
    b) A Born (in London) B 1986 C 1991 D 1993 E (Signed as) full professional for Manchester United F 2003

8   a) Good points: fun to explore; publicity for new single
       Bad points: exploits son; expensive
    b) i) Feels it's a very successful publicity stunt. – Anna
       ii) Likes the site but sees a fault with it. – Simona
       iii) Thinks it's just a heartless way to make money. – Tony

9   i) DS ii) T iii) T iv) F v) F vi) F vii) DS viii) T ix) F

10 a) time b) dress c) white d) yellow e) plumper
    f) flowers

Pages 14–17: Understanding what the writer 'suggests' (L5–6)

1   a) Yes   b) No

2   a) *Any two of:* 'concentrated entirely', 'without spilling a drop', 'exactly equal numbers', 'precise centre', 'carried it so carefully'
    b)–c) *Check your answer with your teacher.*

3   *Check your answer with your teacher.*

4   C, B, A, E, F, D

5–7 *Check your answer with your teacher.*

Pages 18–21: Understanding what the writer 'suggests' (L6–7)

8   a) said Holmes cheerily; This is my intimate friend and associate, Dr Watson, to light the fire. Pray draw up to it; order you a cup of hot coffee
    b) *Check your answer with your teacher.*

9   *Sample answer:*
    Sherlock Holmes seems to be a very intelligent, observant person. While he is talking to the woman, he seems to take note of everything about her in 'one of his quick, all-comprehensive glances'. Also, he cleverly works out how she had arrived by noticing the return train ticket she was holding. He manages to do that and, at the same time, he can be sympathetic and thoughtful. He realises the woman is upset and tries to calm her by talking 'soothingly' and 'patting her forearm'.

10 a) inky b) A to iii; B to iv; C to i; D to ii

11 *Sample answer:*
    You know that his fear about the bears was so strong because it says it kept him awake 'night after night'. He says it was almost like an obsession and that reinforces the idea that the fear was so powerful that he couldn't seem to get rid of it. His wakefulness is conveyed by the description of him 'staring' at the ceiling instead of sleeping. You could think that he is wide-eyed with fear as he thinks of the bears. His imagination was so 'vivid' that it kept him awake and the real tree shadows on his ceiling transported him to the darkness of the forest and prevented him from sleeping.

Pages 22–25: Commenting on text organisation (L5–6)

1   'You're only a few clicks away from providing the support that could change someone's life.'; 'Giving regularly really is the best way to support Oxfam.'; 'What can you buy for 16p a day?'

2   a) Level 5 b) Level 6 c) Level 5 d) Level 6

3   The biggest figure comes first because the writer wants to highlight that most of the money donated is spent helping people.

4   a) 'Uncle took me to market and sold me'
    b) They are both about Lu Si-yan being taken to the market.
    c) To shock and interest the reader.

5   para 2 – D, B; para 3 – A, C

6   Increases tension as reader is more alert or suspicious of other characters' actions.

7   *Sample answer:*
    1 introduces idea/suggests a problem
    2 describes conditions at sea
    3 gives family background
    4 shows how bleak home is

8   *Sample answer:*
    Writer unveils a little information in each paragraph to interest reader and to build a picture of the boy's life. This provides the reader with enough information to *know* that

he will go to sea whether his father wants him to or not.

Pages 26–29: Commenting on text organisation (L6–7)

9 a)–b) *Check your answer with your teacher.*
10 a) I b) C c) C
11 a)

Evidence		Explanation
Paragraph 1	**Paragraph 2**	
not stupid	sublime skill	Builds up respect for Hamilton by repeating a reference to his skill or intelligence.
the trickiest conditions	turn out to be perfect	Underlines the tricky driving conditions and his success.
luck	accidentally	Stresses how it was all a matter of chance.
Fortunately for Hamilton	did him a favour	Emphasises hw lucky he was.
when it rains	A light shower	Reminds the reader of the weather conditions during the race.

b) *Sample answer:*

In the first paragraph the writer stresses that it was a difficult race because he says it took place in the 'trickiest' of conditions. He then hints that it was 'luck' that was the main reason for Hamilton's victory. That helps to make more sense of the opening sentence and you realise that Hamilton is clever enough to recognise how fortunate he was. The second paragraph emphasises the tricky conditions by describing the 'slippery' surface in more detail. Also the idea of how lucky Hamilton was is dealt with in more detail. Hamilton's 'sublime skill' is recognised but the writer stresses that would have counted for nothing until a lucky accident 'did him a favour'. It all builds up and shows the difficulty of winning in conditions like that.

Pages 30–33: Commenting on the writer's use of language (L5–6)

1 a) repetition – 'a man';
a list – 'soaked in water, and smothered in mud, and lamed by stones, and cut by flints, and stung by nettles, and torn by briars'/'who limped, and shivered, and glared and growled; alliteration – 'glared and growled'/'soaked' and 'smothered'
b) To make the man seem frightening a bit like an animal.
c) glared and growled
d) *Check your answer with your teacher.*
2 a)–d) *Check your answer with your teacher.*
3 a) yellow b) green c)/d) light/interesting
e)/f) slower/clumsier
4 a)–b) *Check your answer with your teacher.*

Pages 34–37: Commenting on the writer's use of language (L6–7)

5 a) not destroyed – not dulled – Repetition of 'not' and the 'd' sound b) Emphasises firmness of his belief he's not mad.
a) heaven/hell – Contrast b) *Check your answer with your teacher.*
a) I am mad?/am I mad? – Repetition of question b) Stresses idea of madness.
6 *Check your answer with your teacher.*
7 a)–b) *Check your answer with your teacher.*
8 a) Uses contrasts between success and failure, e.g. real loser/adoring public.
b) *Check your answer with your teacher.*
9 a)–b) *Check your answer with your teacher.*

Pages 38–41: Commenting on the writer's viewpoint and purpose (L5–6)

1 a) *Check your answer with your teacher.*
b) correct c) Level 5
2 a)–e) True
3–5 *Check your answer with your teacher.*
6 a) short b) describes c) real d) last
e) impression
7 a) negative b) 'sharp-faced'/'tight little mouth'/'curved downwards'
c) *Check your answer with your teacher.*
8 *Check your answer with your teacher.*

Pages 42–45: Commenting on the writer's viewpoint and purpose (L6–7)

9 a) *Check your answer with your teacher.*
b) i) glories and luxuries, good food and teaching, fine uniforms
ii) the knowledge and skill of the white man
10 a)–c) Y
11–12 *Check your answer with your teacher.*
13 a) *Check your answer with your teacher.*
b) quotation/analysis/explanation
c) *Check your answer with your teacher.*
d) *Sample answers:*
The school seems to be a very friendly place. The head's wife seems very relaxed with the boys and she even jokes with them about the 'lies' they might tell Charles about the food at the school. It seems to be the sort of place where there are no secrets or strict rules. The fact that she says they should tell him 'all' about the school suggests that she feels there is nothing unpleasant to hide about it. The boys' reactions seem to suggest the same thing. They respond to the comment about the food with 'exaggerated' groans, as if they are enjoying the joke. The fact that the groans are 'amiable' stresses

the sense of friendliness. Their faces are 'open' and they treat her with politeness when they 'hold the door' for her. It seems a place of happy, relaxed pupils who know how to have fun, but also how to be respectful.

14 a)–c) *Share ideas with a partner or teacher.*

15 *Sample answer:*

It starts to feel threatening immediately because the boy becomes the centre of attention, but in an unpleasant way. It is as if he is being trapped. The circle of pupils 'contracts' around him like he is being imprisoned or captured. The faces close in and they examine him in a calculating, unpleasant way.

The following paragraph emphasises the questions that are thrown at him. It is as if they are attacking and robbing him when it says 'They help themselves to his name, his age, his school.' He is obviously frightened because he cannot speak and he stands 'humped' as if under a hail of blows. He feels lost and threatened by the noise and it all builds up to a crescendo with quickly repeated questions at the end of the second paragraph.

The final paragraph is literally threatening. The voice carries a fearful message and the school seems to have become a threatening, menacing place.